Ctrl+X
Ctrl+C
Ctrl+V

CUT COPY PASTE

Cut, Copy, Paste is an allegorical appraisal of AI portraiture, modern-insta-faux realist culture. An artistic realisation of how society has devolved to where people have become PICK'N'MIX anatomical distortions. How the unachievable beauty standards of homo digitalis, resulting in physical and digital warping of Vitruvian form. My work reflects this through the Collage of Mona Lisa and Sugar Skulls . The sugar Skulls represents the thin line of life and death we walk to become 'beautiful'. Drawing from Frida Kahlo and my own experiences.

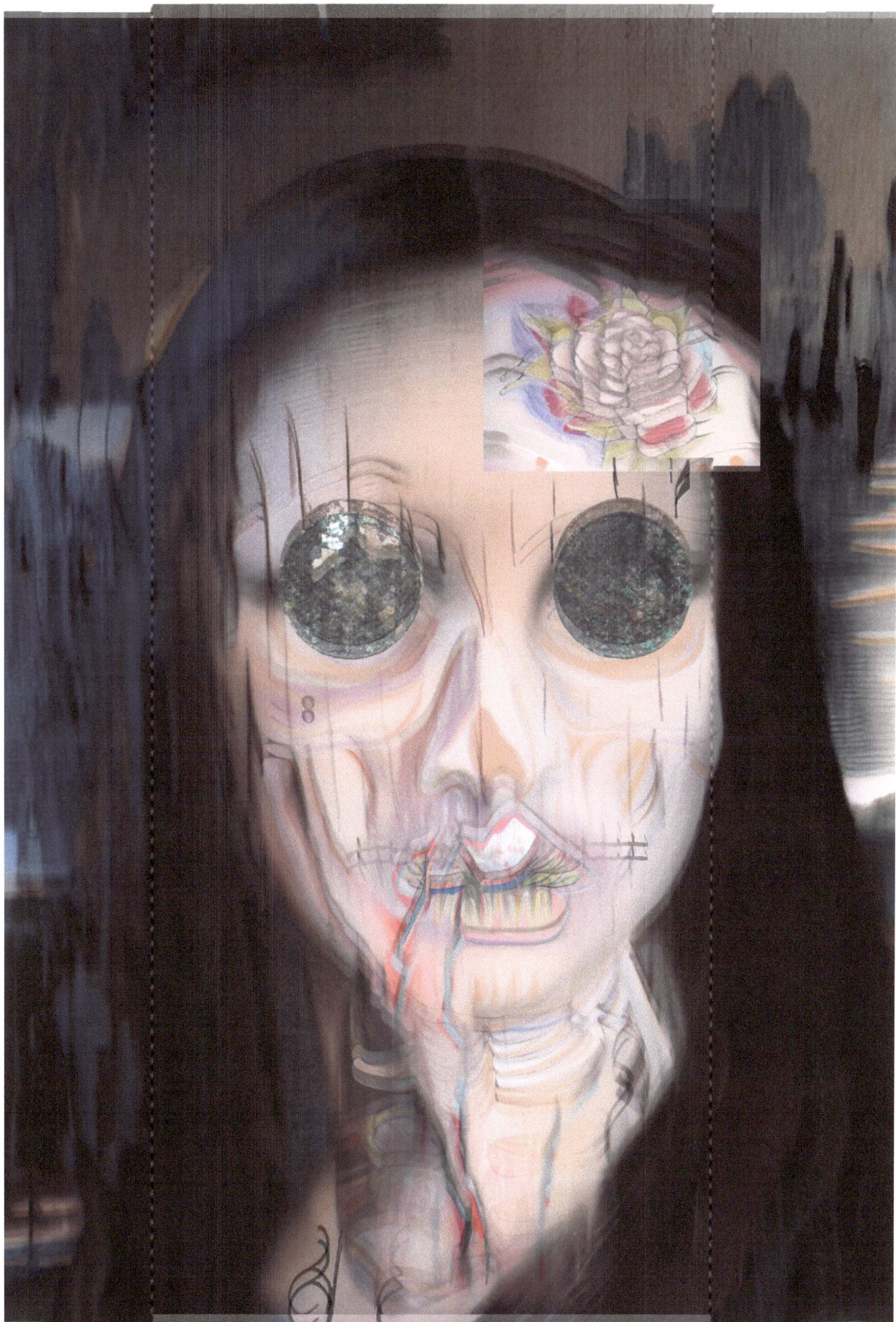

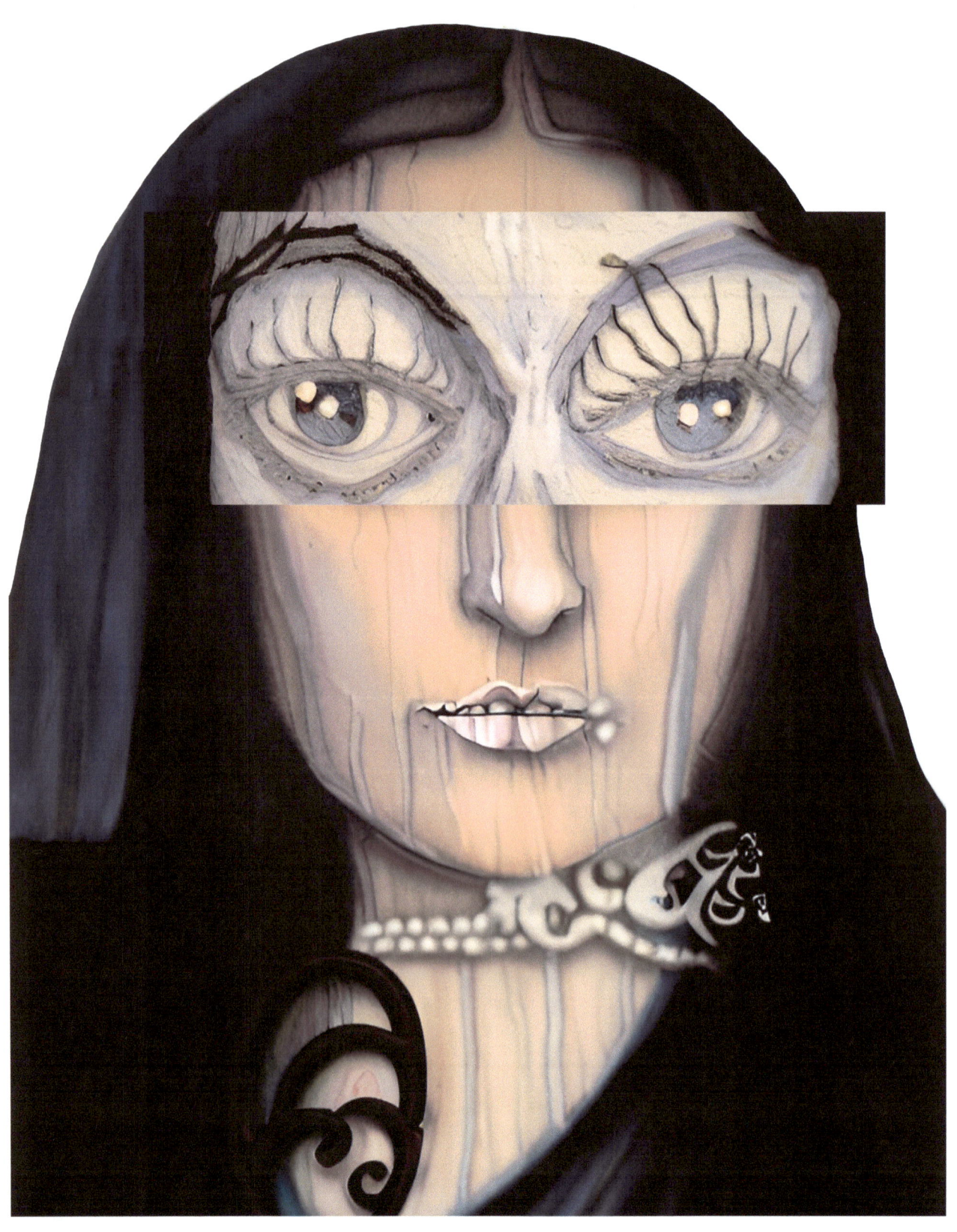

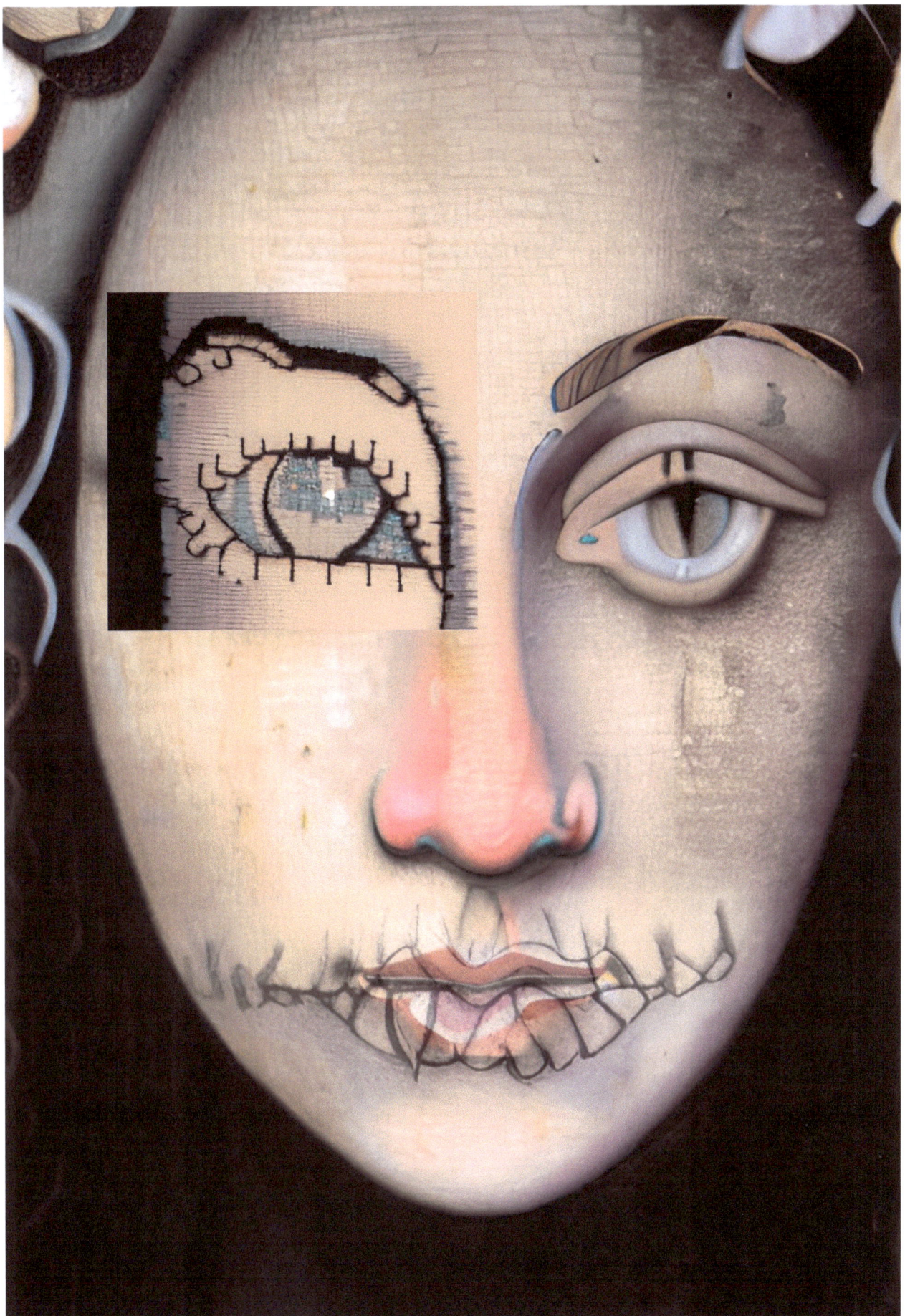

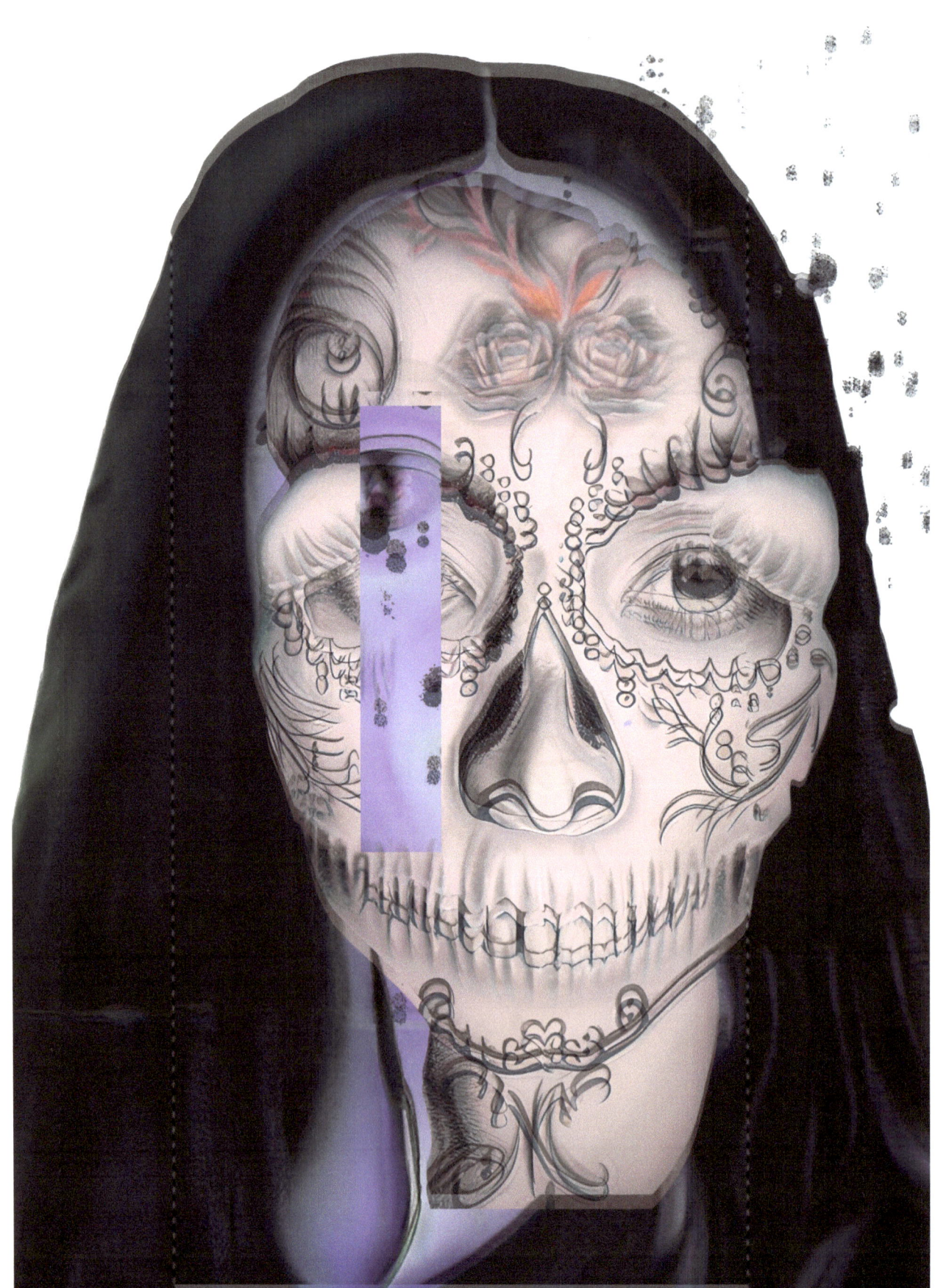

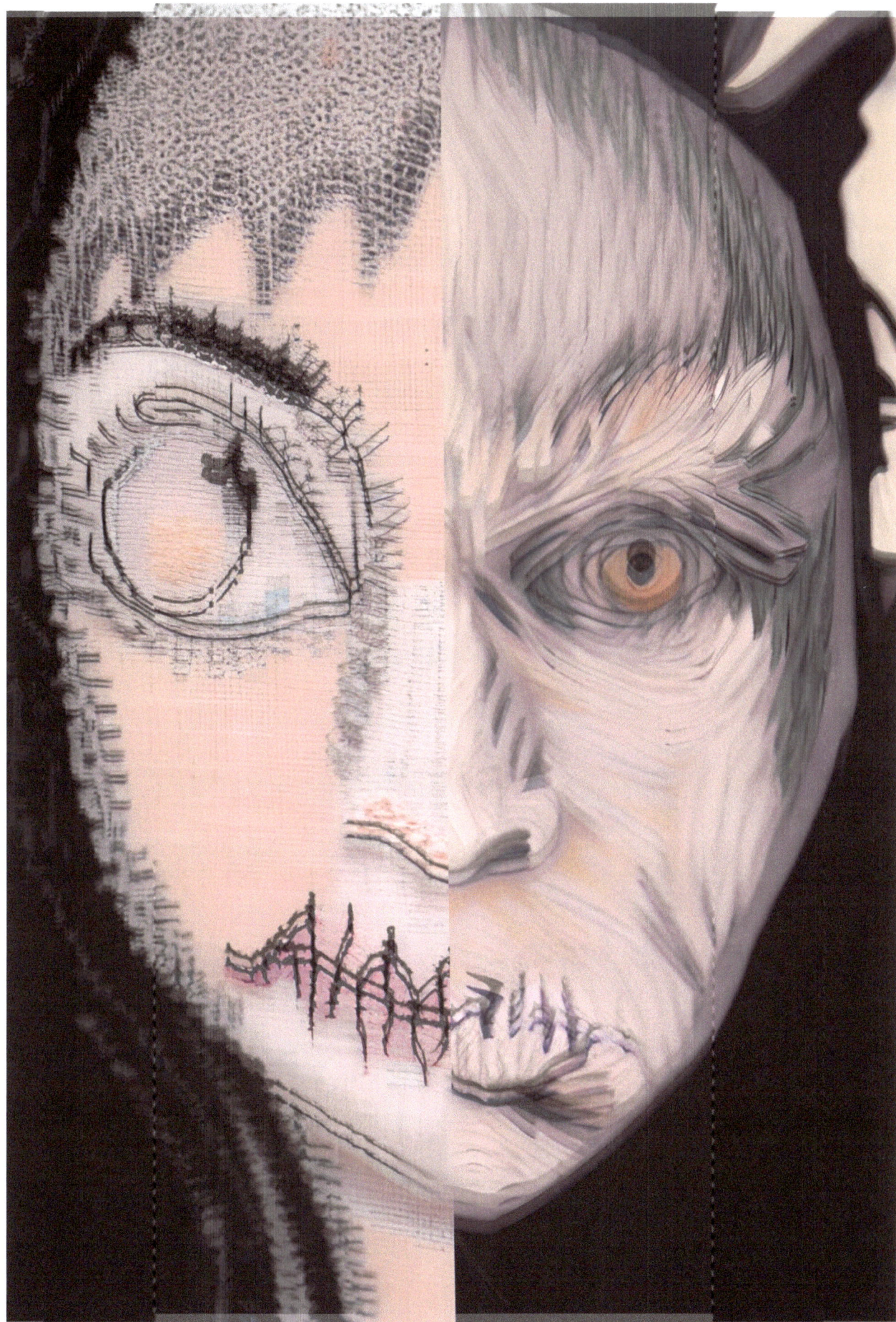

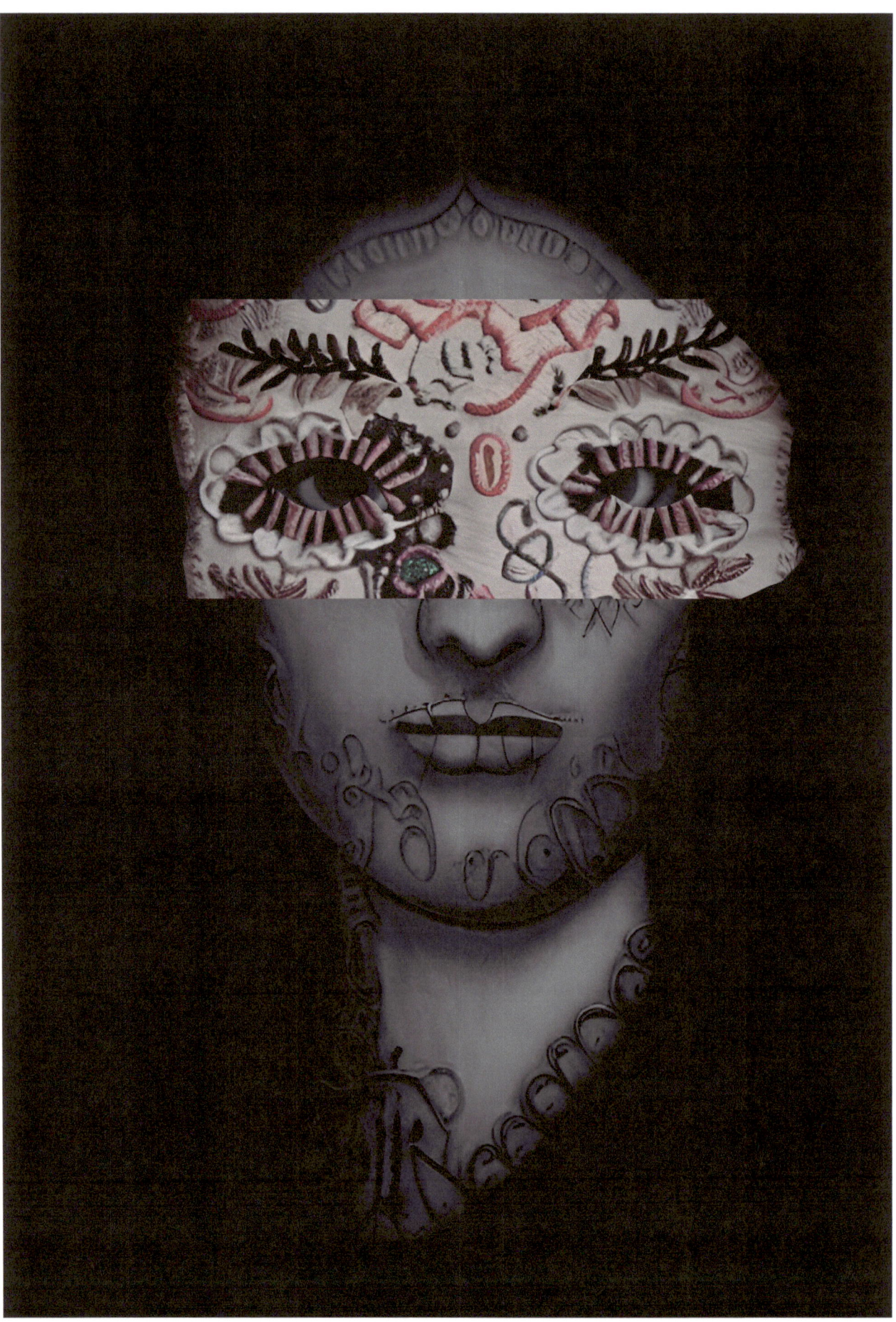

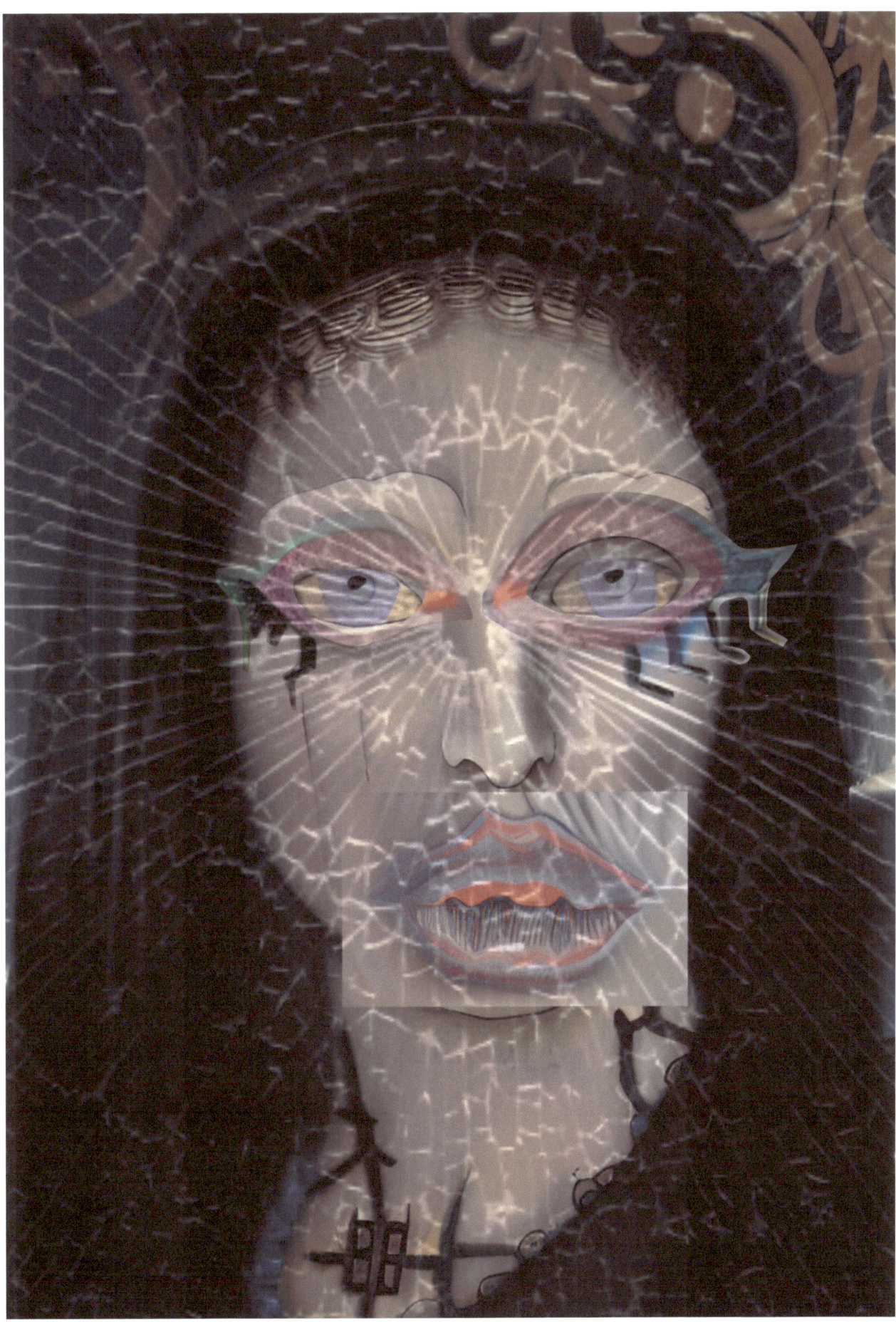

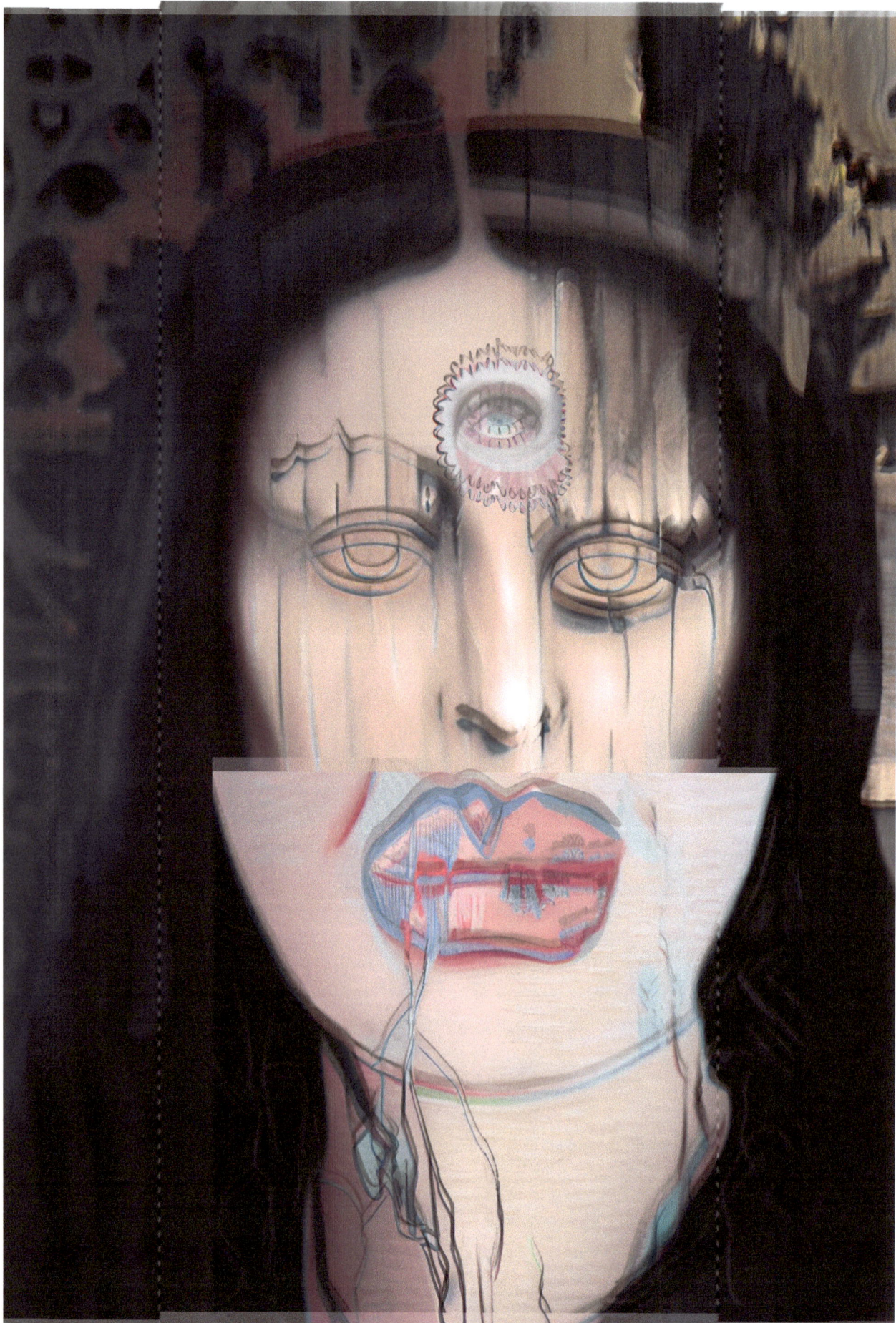

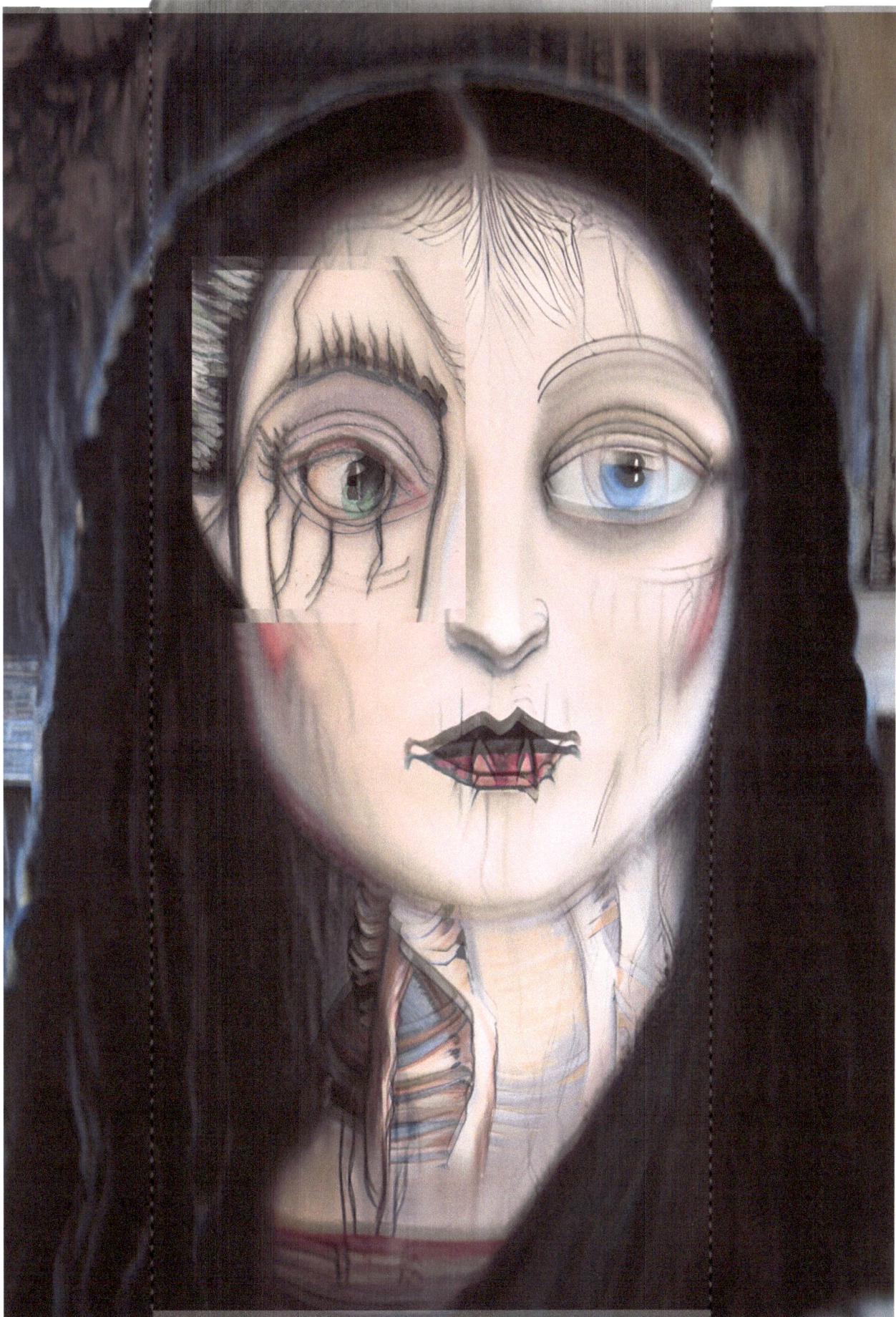

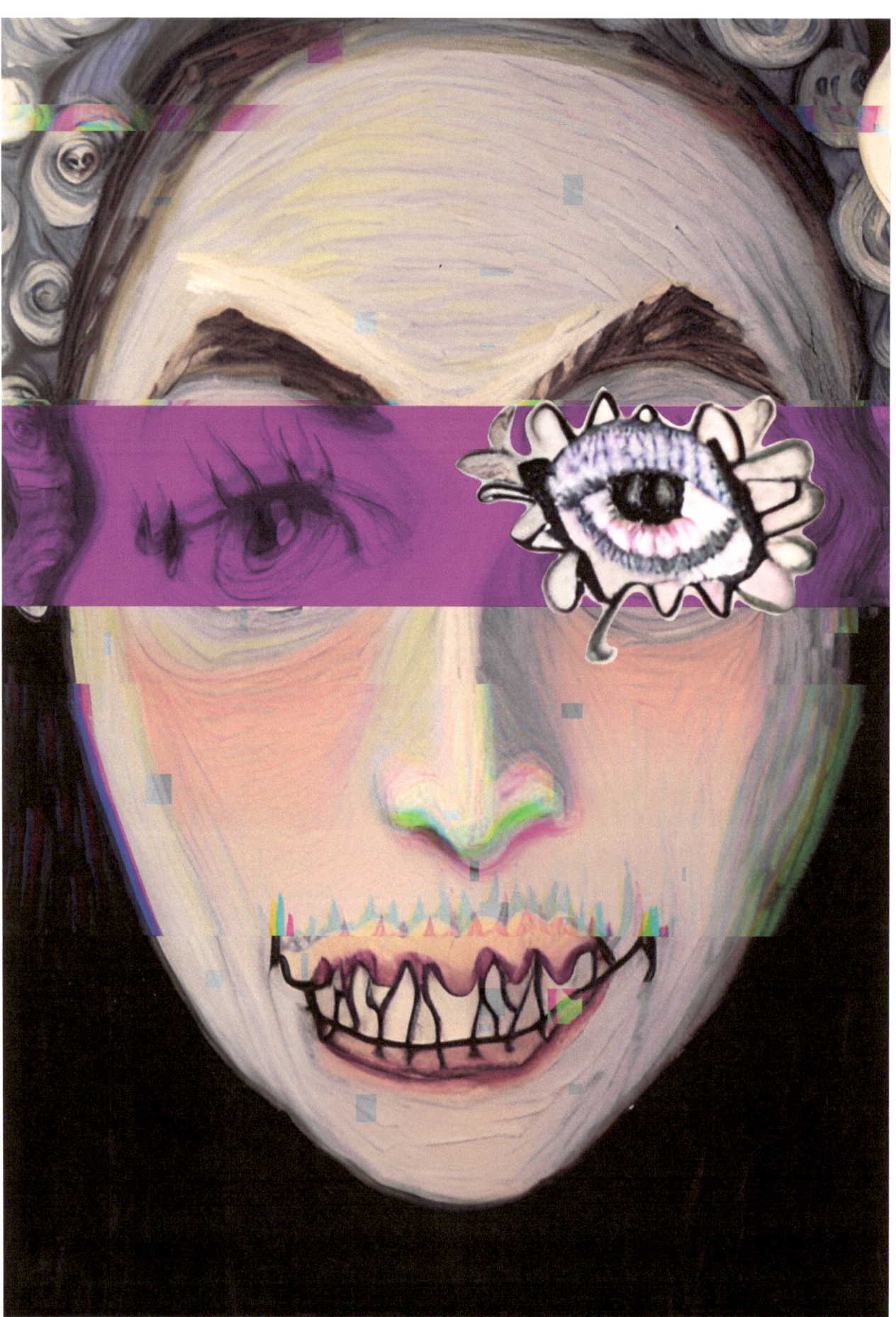

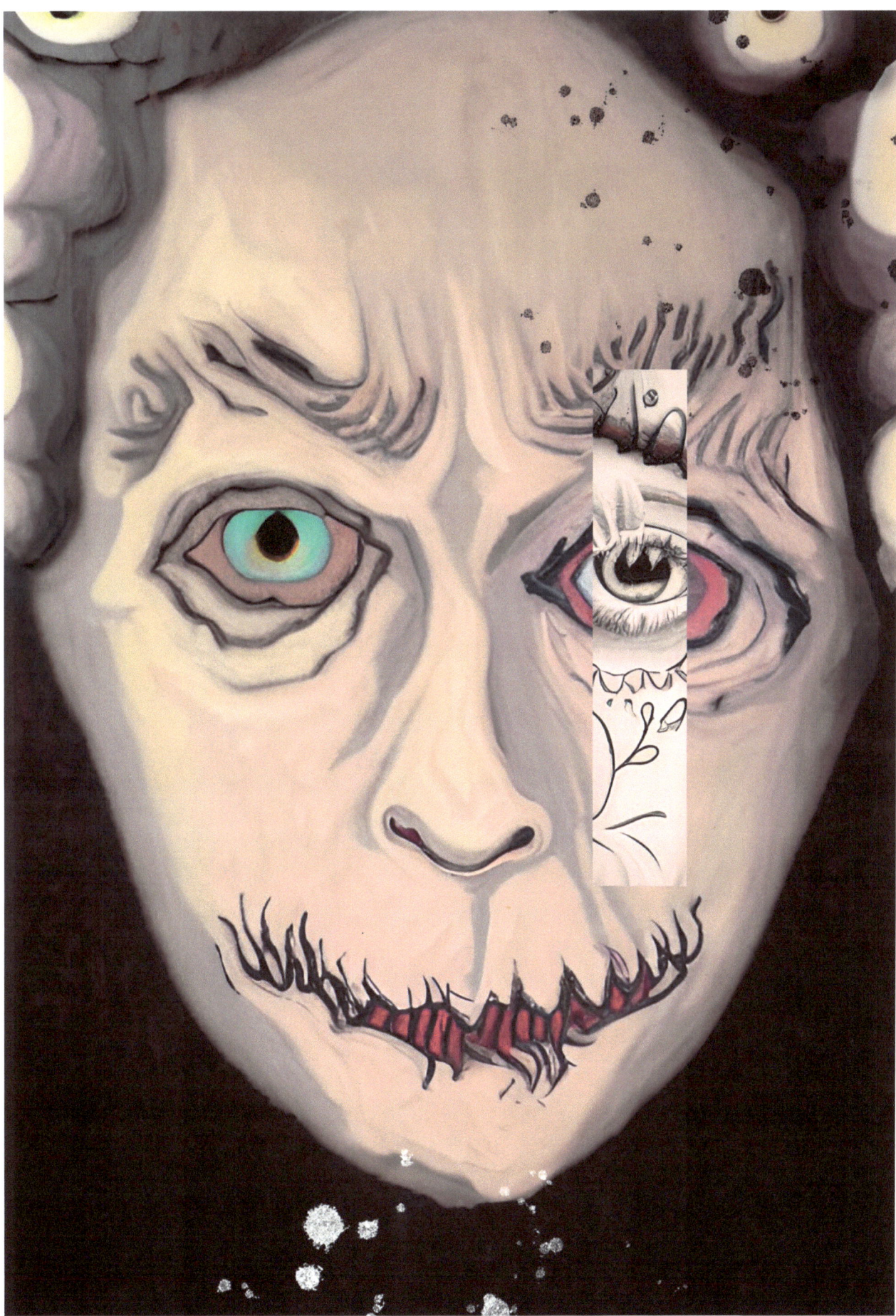

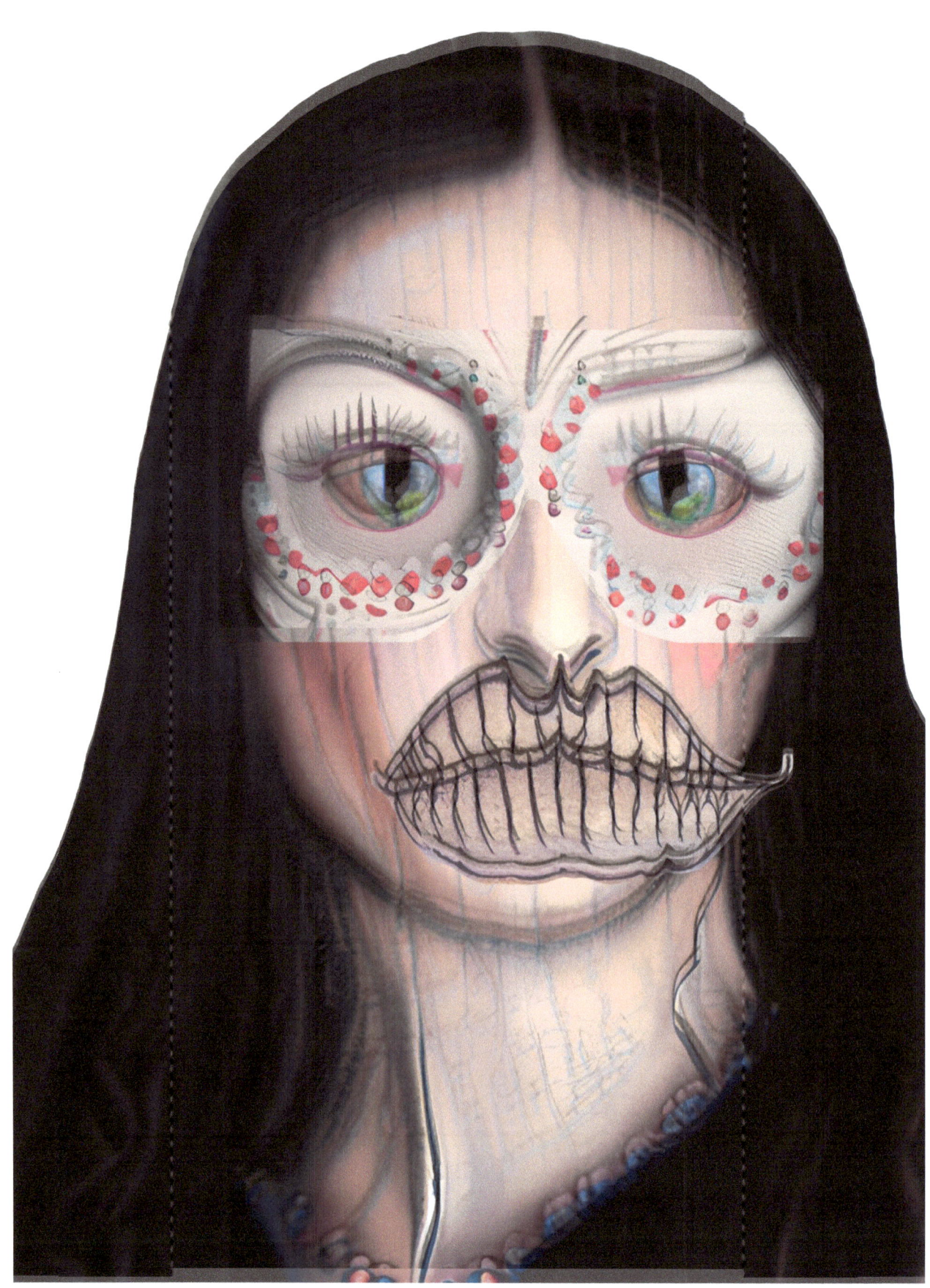

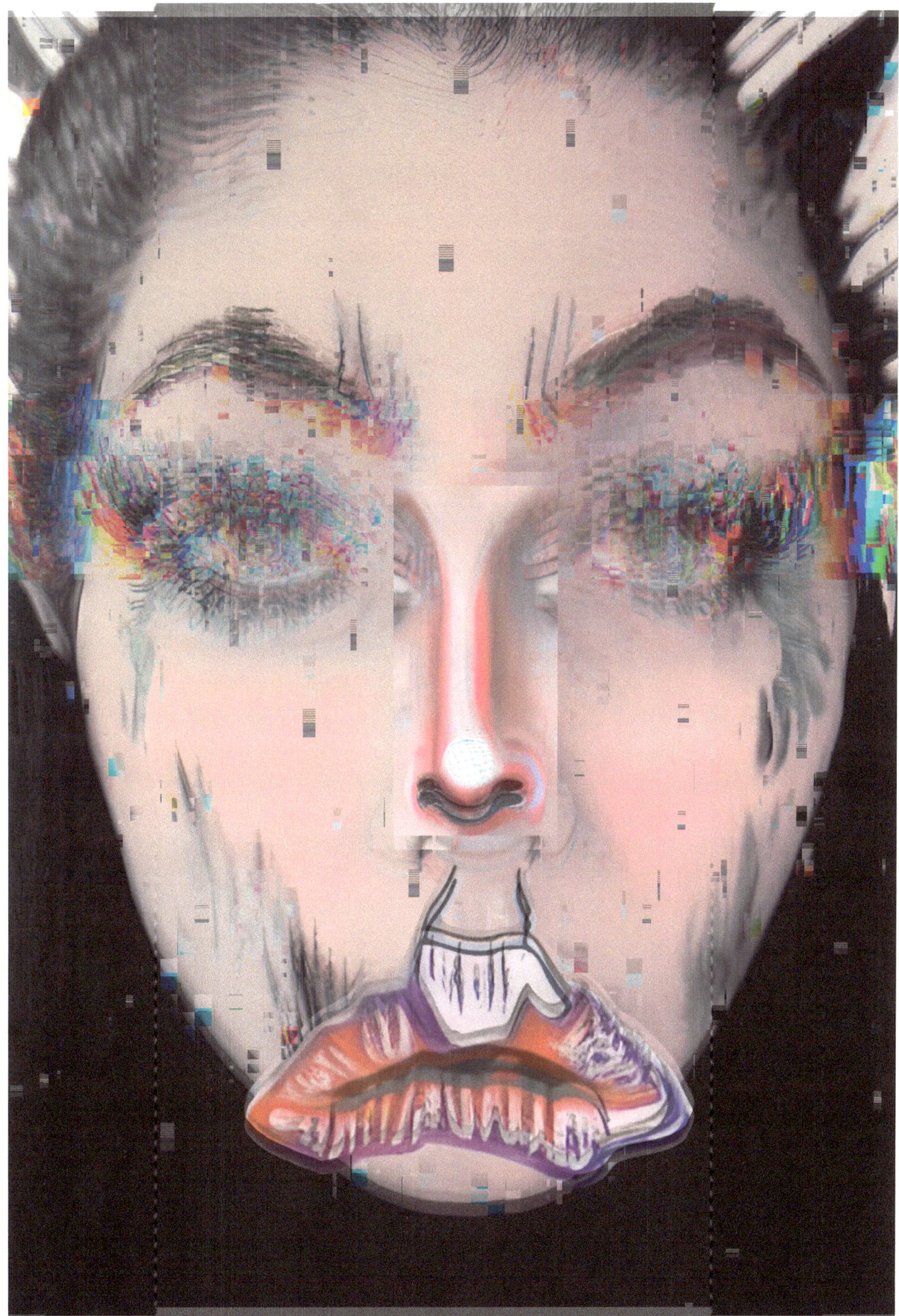

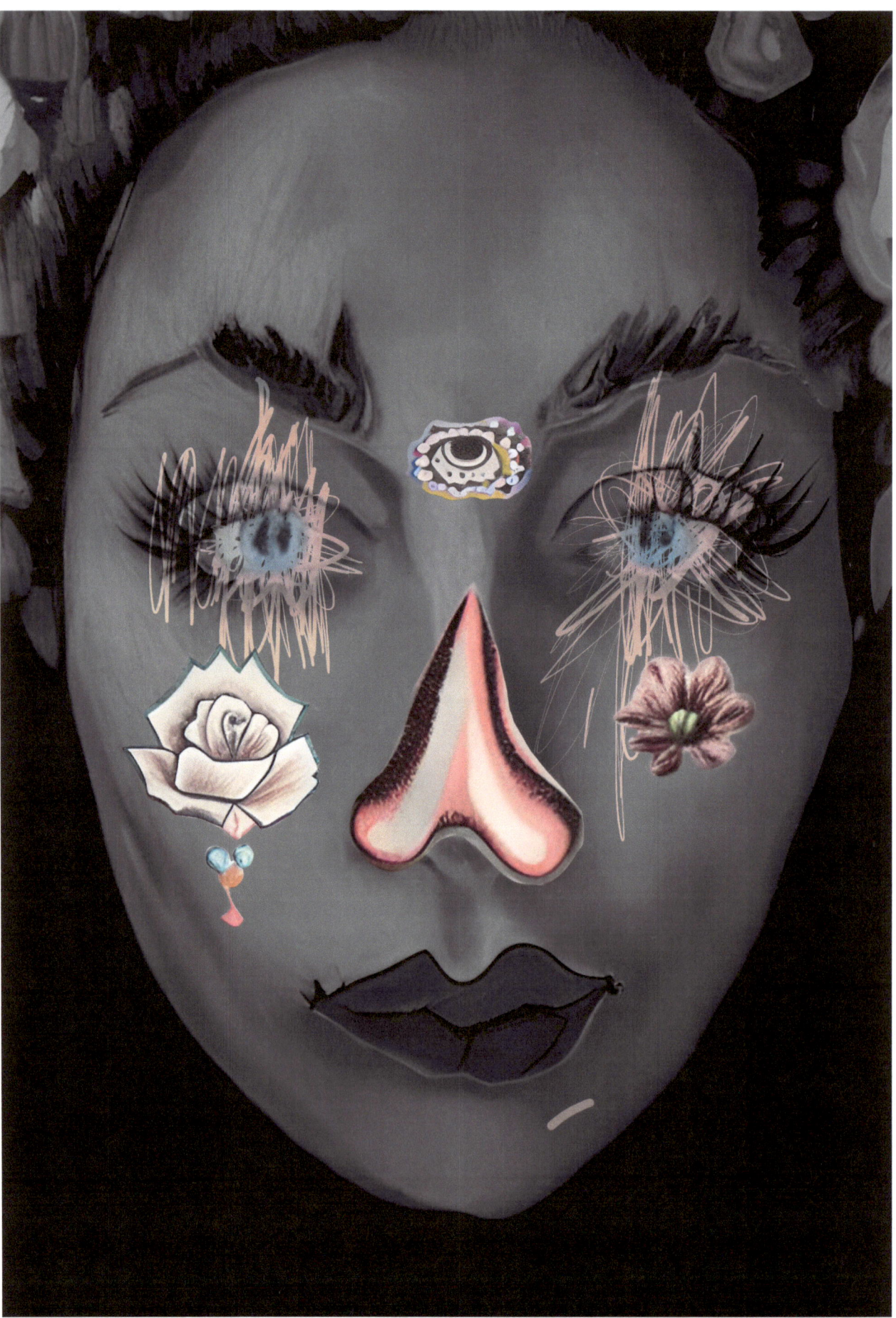

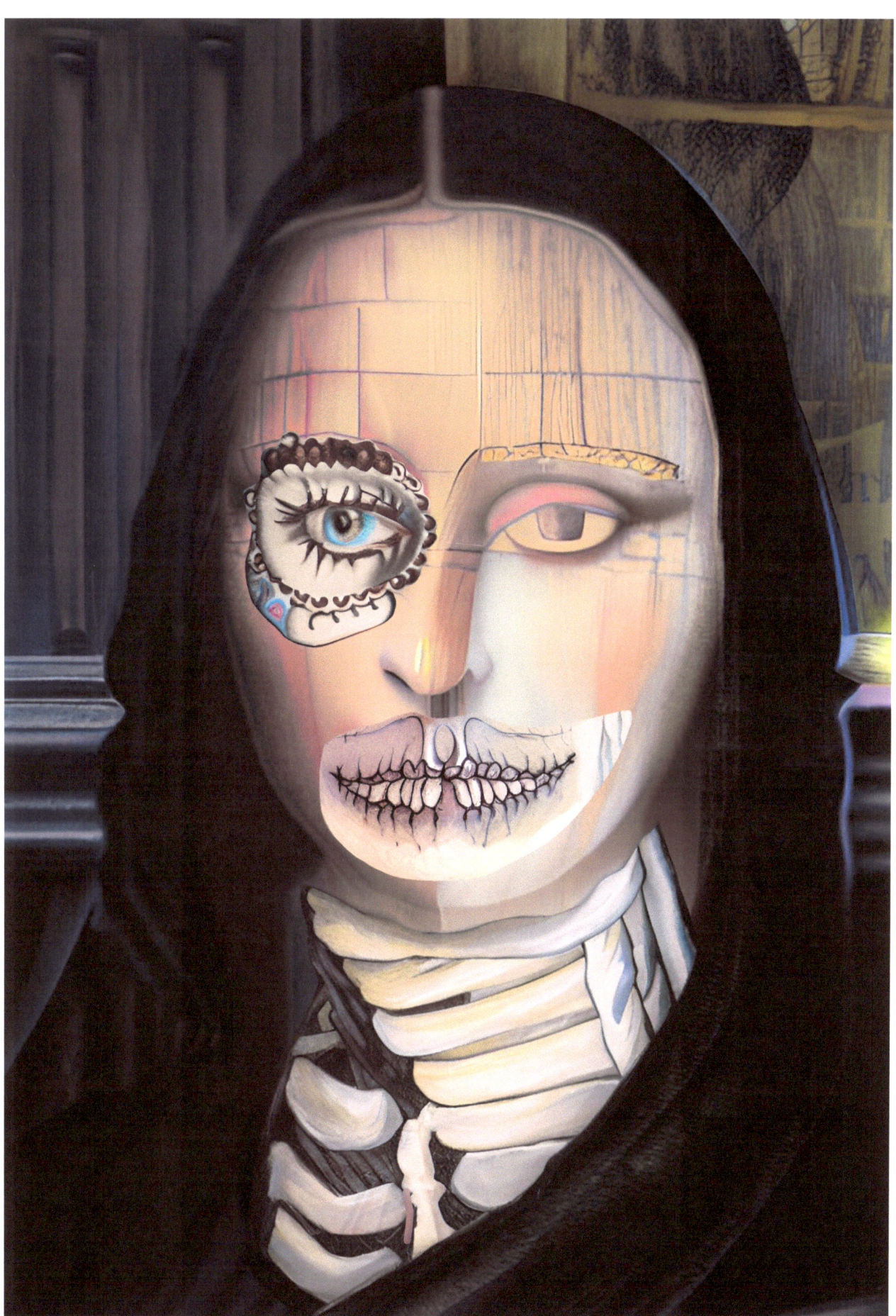

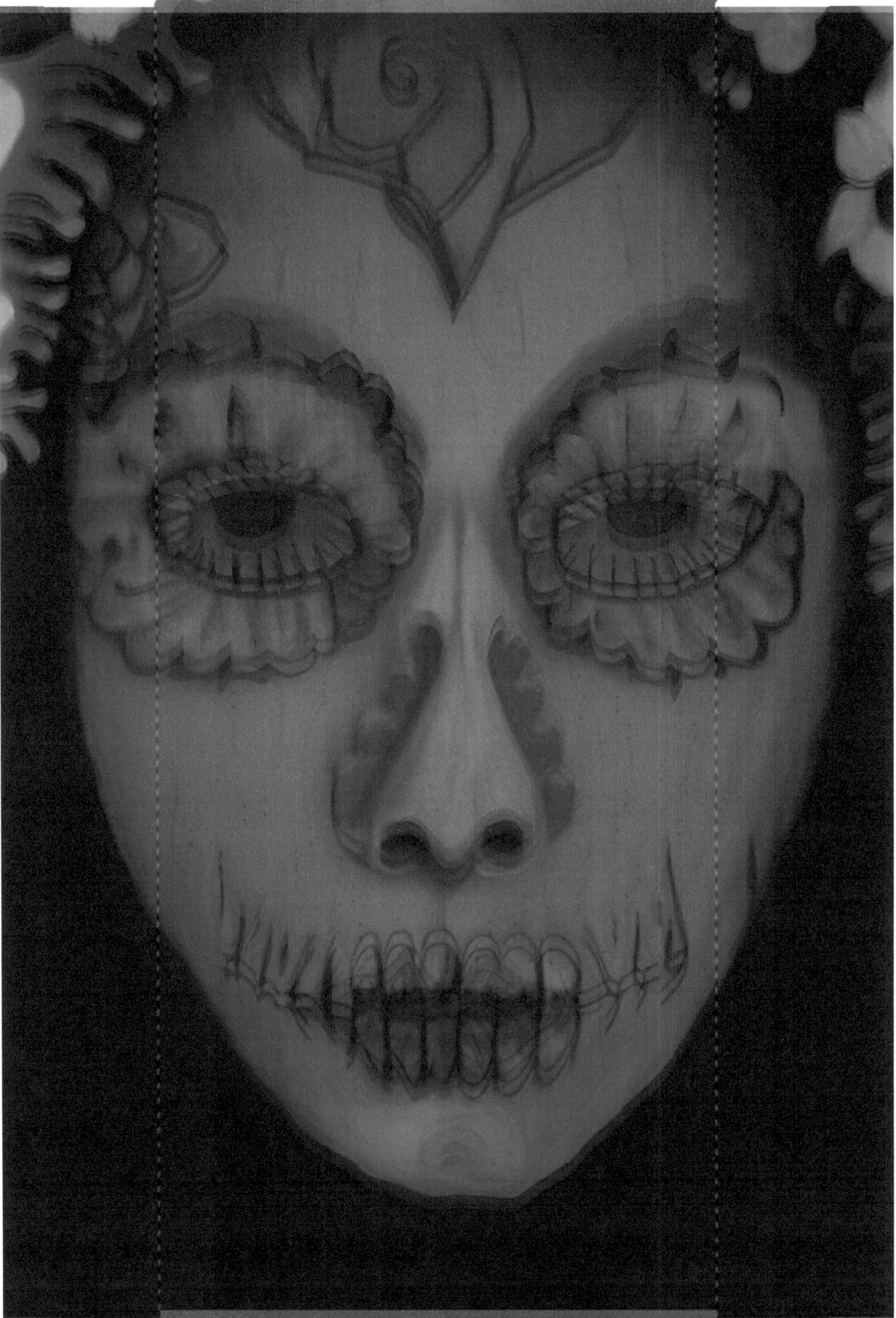

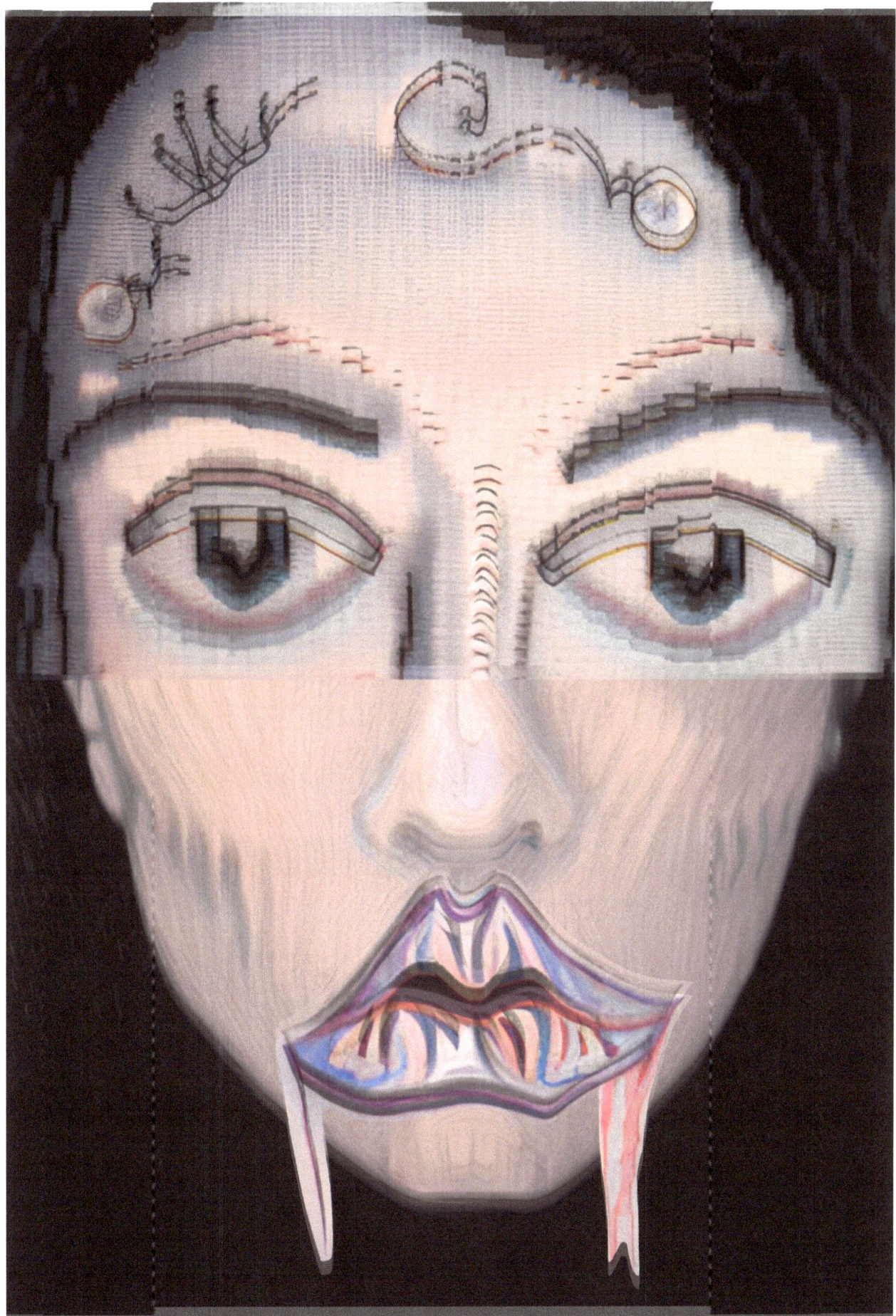

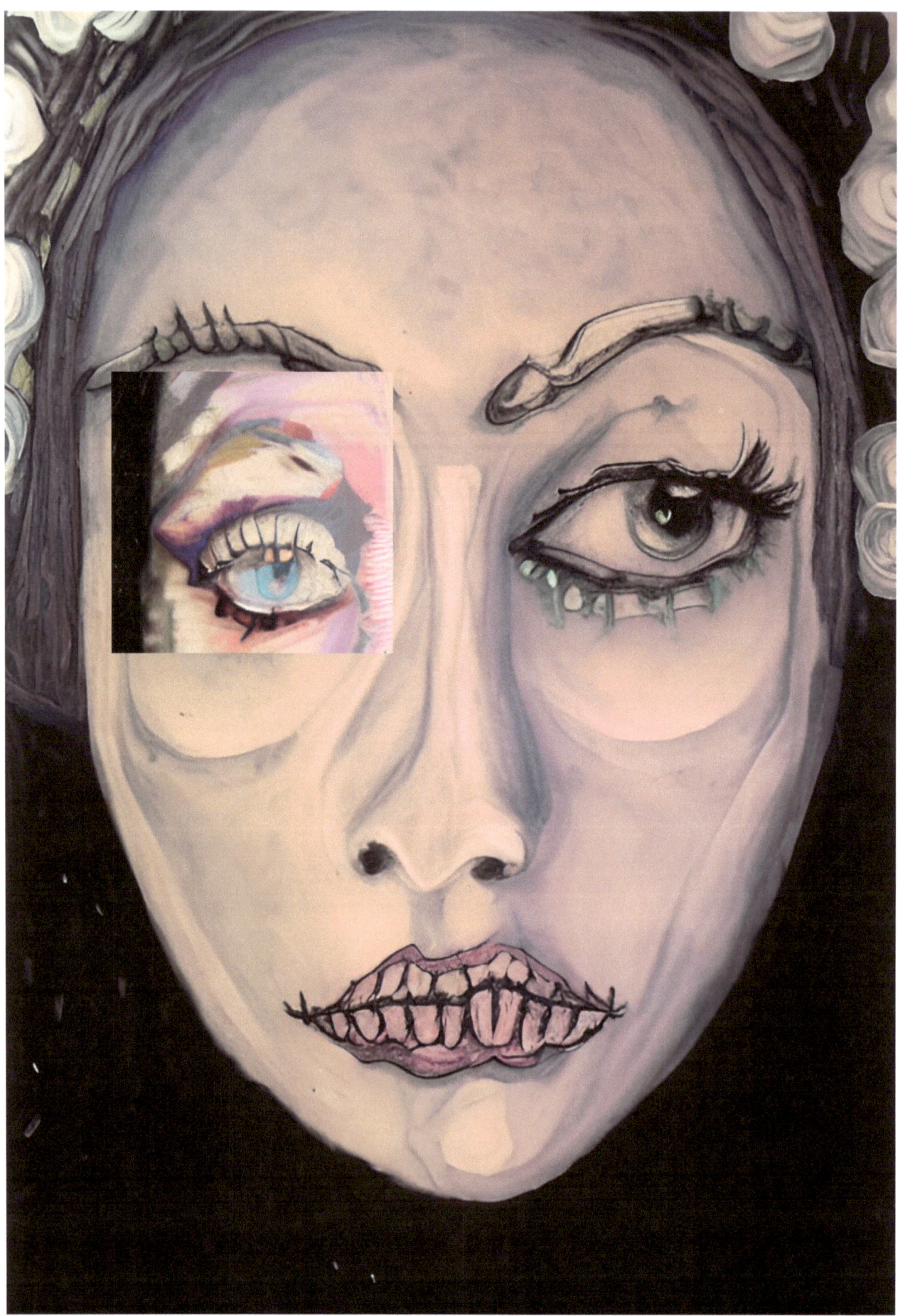

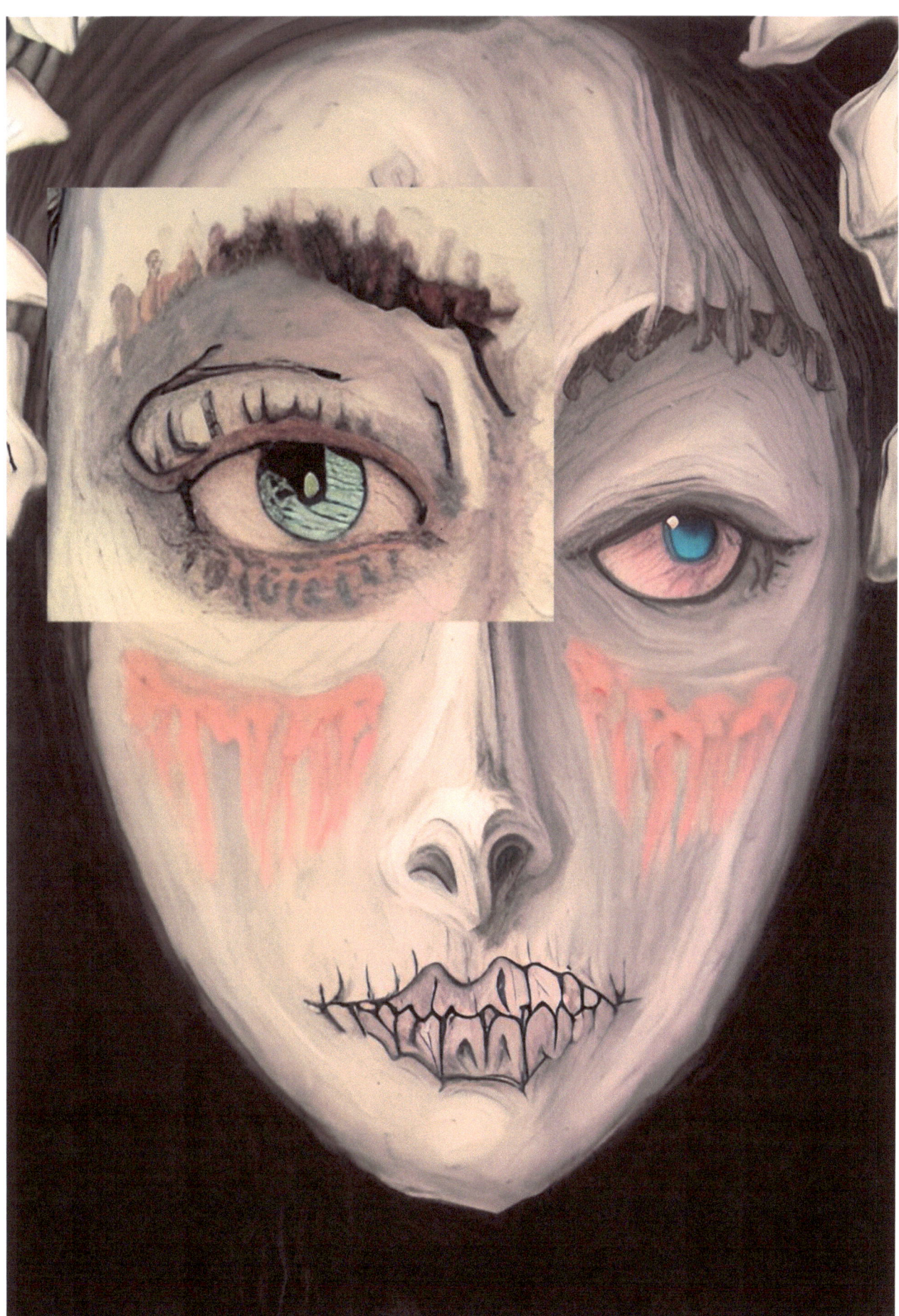

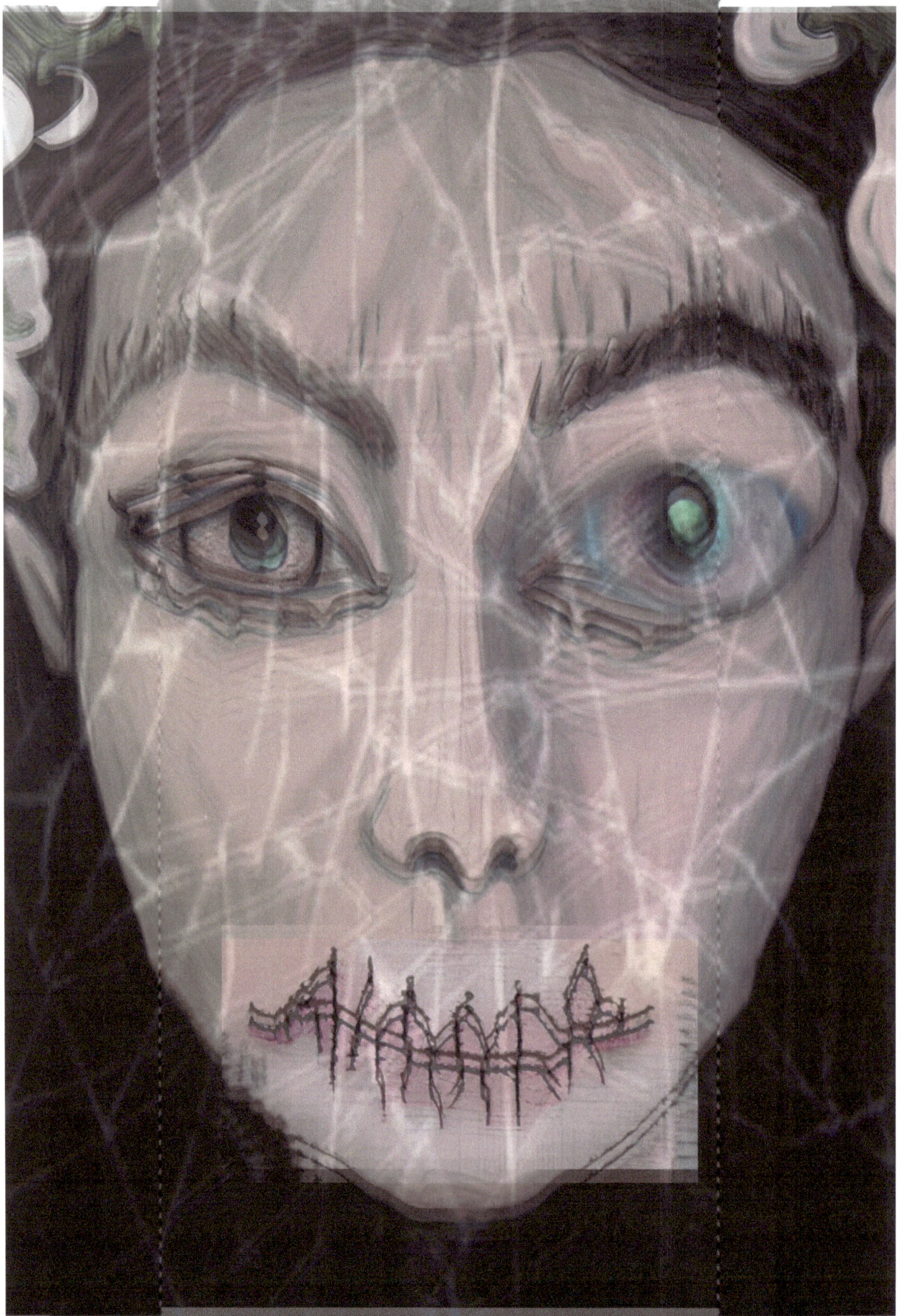

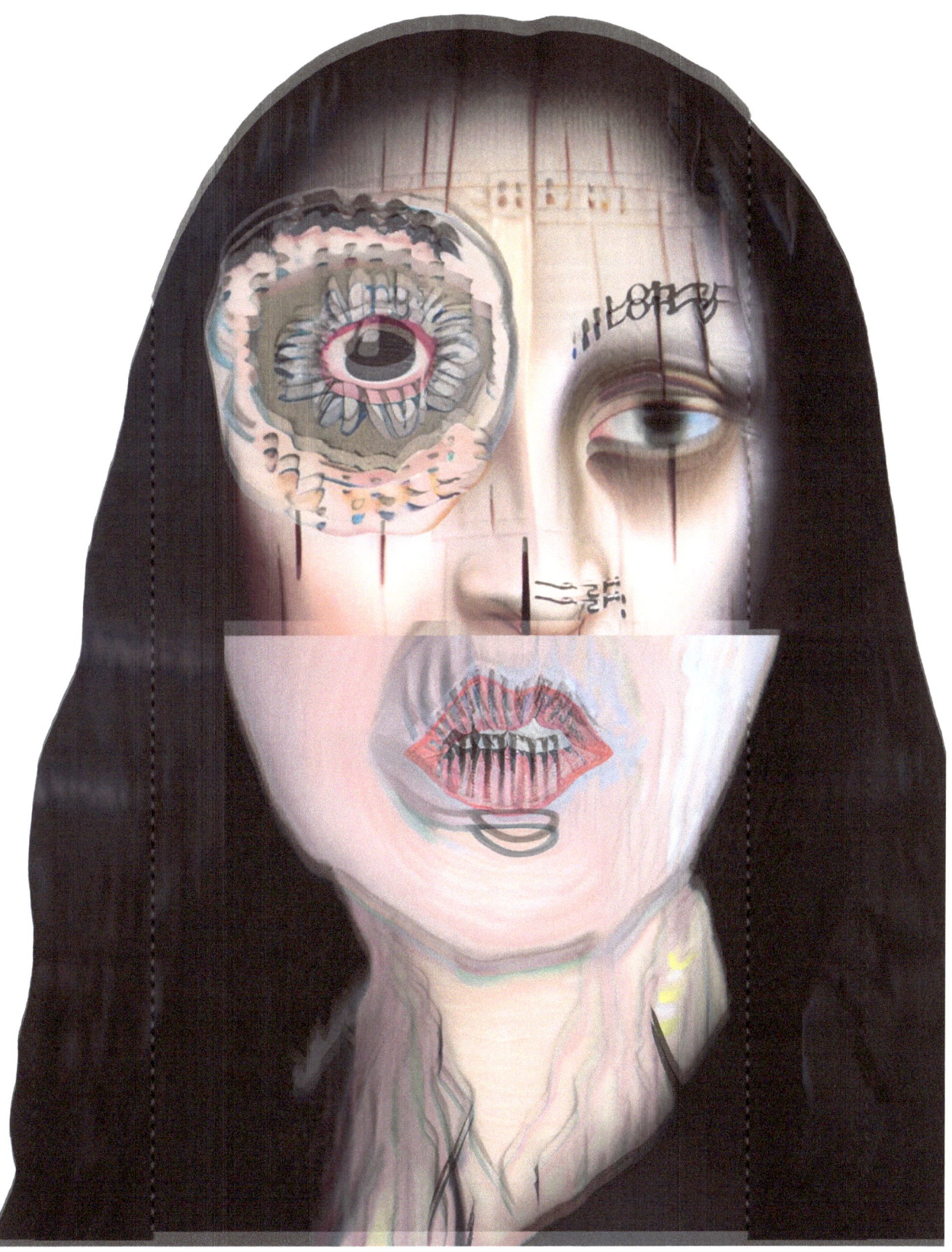

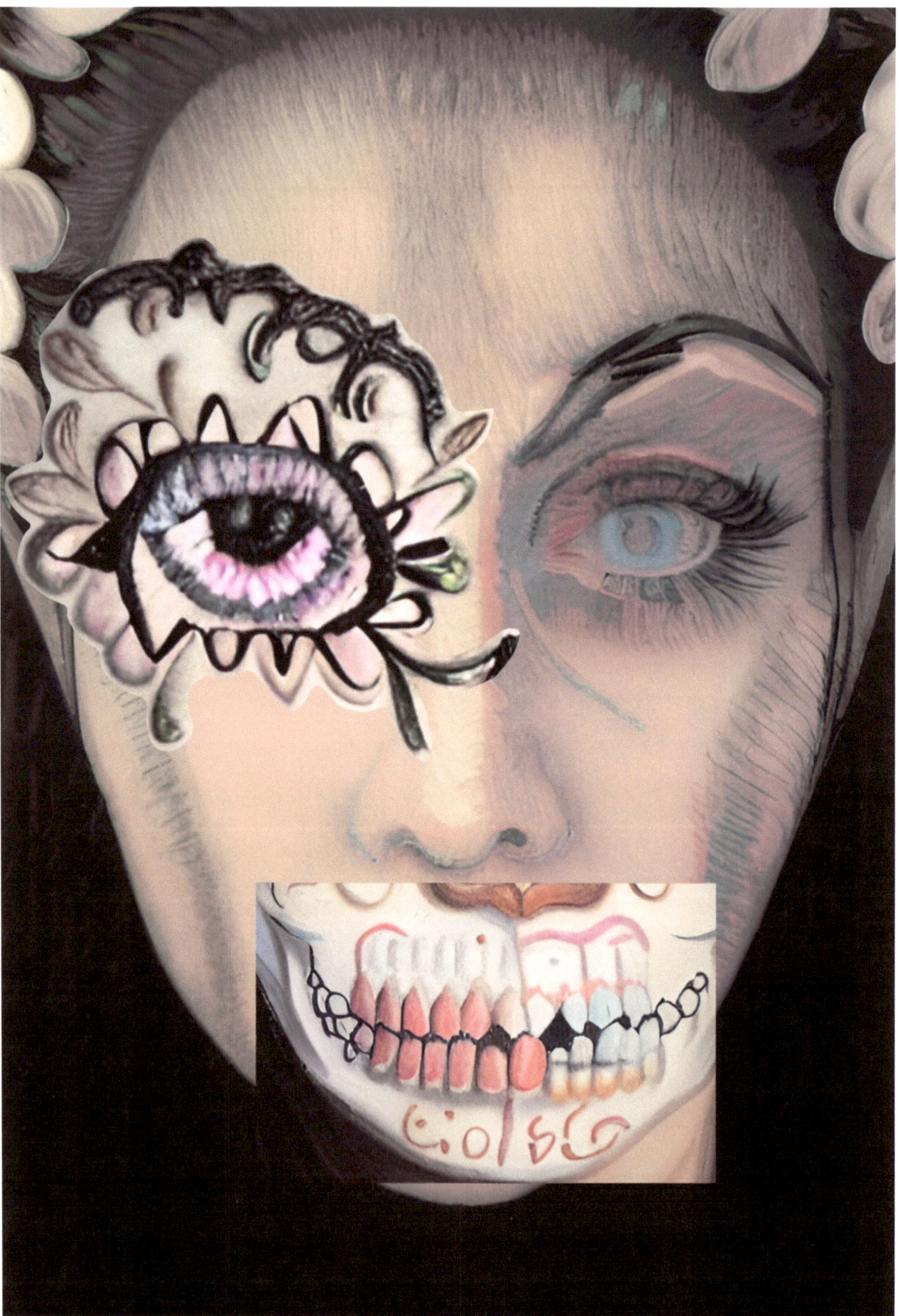

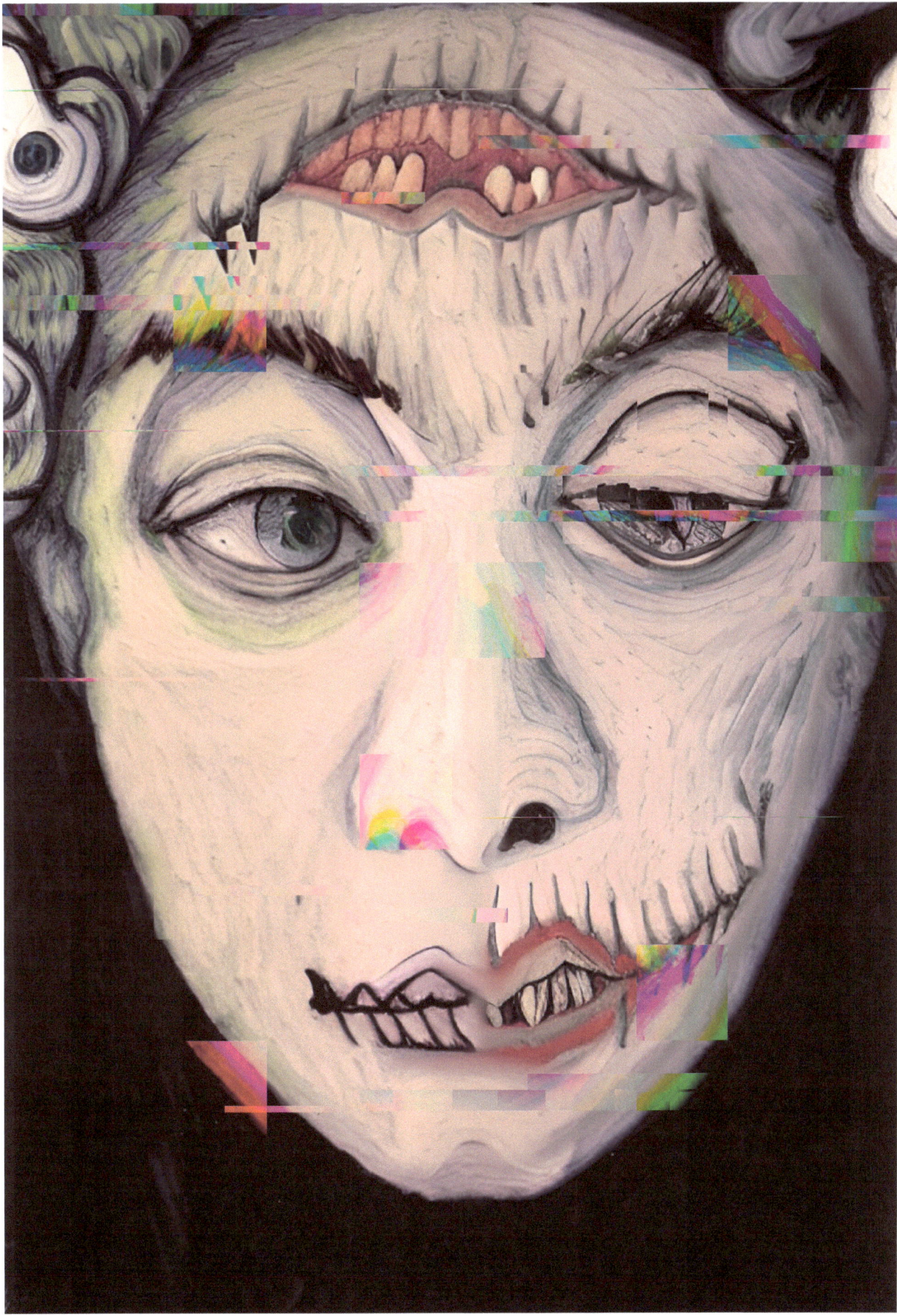

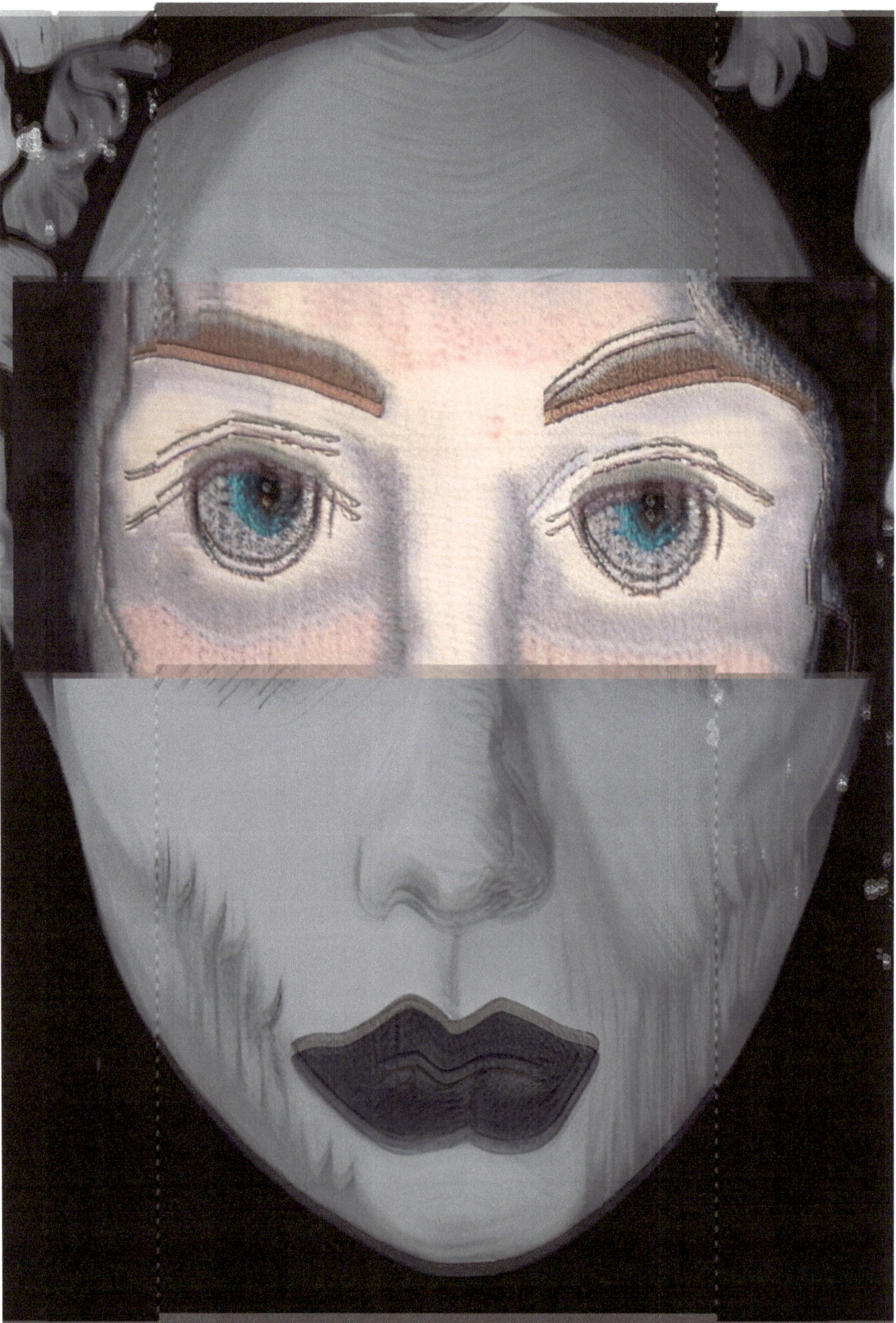

www.ingramcontent.com/pod-product-compliance
Lightning Source LLC
Chambersburg PA
CBHW051953210526
45473CB00024B/2361